IMAGES
of England

ASHINGTON

Ask anyone local: 'Who more than anyone else helped to put the name of Ashington on the map?' And ninety-nine out of a hundred will say 'Jackie Milburn'. Wor Jackie came on the scene soon after the Second World War ended, when people were looking for a folk hero. Jackie came ready made – good looking, athletic, charming, modest and talented. He is seen here being introduced, by Newcastle United captain Joe Harvey, to King George VI, prior to the 1951 FA Cup Final in which Jackie scored both of United's goals in a 2-0 victory over Blackpool.

IMAGES
of England

ASHINGTON

Compiled by
Mike Kirkup

TEMPUS

First published 1999
Reprinted 2000
Copyright © Mike Kirkup, 1999

Tempus Publishing Limited
The Mill, Brimscombe Port,
Stroud, Gloucestershire, GL5 2QG

ISBN 0 7524 1602 2

Typesetting and origination by
Tempus Publishing Limited
Printed in Great Britain by
Midway Clark Printing, Wiltshire

The use of pit ponies was widespread in the Ashington group of collieries. Here Neil Carrick and Tom Rigg take a breather with their white Gallowa in the Plessey Seam of the Duke Pit in the 1960s.

Contents

Acknowledgements   6

Introduction   7

1.   Old Ashington   9

2.   Shops   25

3.   Entertainment   37

4.   Education   49

5.   Recreation   67

6.   Sport   91

7.   Coal   111

Acknowledgements

This book could not have been produced without the hard work of the photographers who captured all aspects of life in and around Ashington over the years. The early photographers were Johnnie Biggs, Alf Jenson, Pentland and Curry; followed by Cuth Stephenson, Bob Johnson and Jackie Laws. Later came the likes of Jack Wallace, Reuben Daglish, Bill Harrison and Jim Brooks, all intent on keeping history alive by capturing groups of people and the changes to buildings. To these can be added the various photographic societies and their members such as Bob Hostler, Mike Parker and Ron Staines. Thanks also to individuals, too numerous to mention, who have provided personal photographs, and to Woodhorn Colliery Museum for access to their archives.

Introduction

The Industrial Revolution of the nineteenth century shaped both the landscape of Ashington and the lifestyle of its inhabitants. Prior to this, the few village residents had huddled together for warmth and security in their tied cottages next to one of the mere half a dozen farms in the vicinity.

Lying sixteen miles north of Newcastle upon Tyne, Ashington's strength was always destined to lie, not in historic buildings or scenic beauty, but in its people, the canny folk who worked long and hard in an effort to put Ashington on the map. Yet until the pits arrived, no cartographer even bothered to include the village in the map of Northumberland! However, that changed when entrepreneurs moved in, howked great holes into the green fields, and decreed that Ashington should be the biggest mining village in the world.

That village soon became a town with all the trappings of an urban district council. Fifty candidates stood in 1896 for the first election of councillors, and the first chairman was Edmund O. Southern, a coal company director who lived later at North Seaton Hall. At their second meeting the council debated the format of a seal for the local authority's headed paper. It was decided that the seal should incorporate a picture of the Duke Pit headgear with the inscription 'Labour Conquers All' ... in Latin. Signs of culture already!

The Reverend J.E. Gordon Cartlidge, vicar of St John's church, Seaton Hirst, highlighted the problems facing the first council in those early days: 'It is difficult to realise the arduous task – poor roads, ash footpaths, little lighting, pools of water all over the place where ashes were worn down or washed away, open ashpits, earth closets, no Picture Palaces, no public park, no buses – and yet there was an amazing friendliness wherever you went. It was a grand life; the work was constructive; we were creating something: the spiritual and cultural life of a new community, and we were trying to keep it Christian against tremendous odds. There were difficulties enough, but there were golden opportunities and we seized them.'

The 'new community' in Ashington was a rare mixture. Most counties in England were represented: tin miners from Cornwall, lead miners from Cumbria, coalminers from Durham whose own pits had closed. All were intent on making a new life for themselves and their families. Irish men and women, who had abandoned their native isle during the potato famine, discovered pots of gold – black gold – on every corner-end in Ashington. Italians found that the local children were ready-made customers for their particular brand of ice-cream and fish and chips. After the Second World War yet another ingredient was added to the Geordie pot when a large Polish contingent settled in town. Little wonder that the broad Ashington accent reflects this heady concoction.

With the influx of people came the mushrooming of houses; colliery rows, back-to-back, built within spitting distance of the pityard. Amenities were few and wages were kept pitifully low. But the miner accepted his lot, not knowing his true worth to the coalmine owners or the country. That was to come with the conflicts of two world wars. When the government of the day shouted out for coal to fuel its munition factories, trains and ships, their plea did not fall on deaf ears. The Ashington miners responded, to a man. But when the time came to give the miners a lift, a helping hand, then political backs were turned.

With the growth in population came the need for more shops, more schools and more places of worship. Soon Ashington spilled over to join Hirst, the division between the two being defined by the railway line. The population grew to almost thirty thousand between the two wars, almost ten thousand of whom worked in the coal trade.

The abstemious Jonathan Priestman, the original Quaker coal owner, died in 1889. Surely it was no coincidence that the town's first two public houses, the Portland and the Grand, were opened soon after, to be followed in quick succession by the first of twenty workingmen's clubs. Ashington became the drink capital of the north east, earning for itself the dubious title of 'Satan's Citadel', a phrase coined by a shocked member of the visiting clergy who also complained: 'During one open-air meeting I even came across a woman who was drunk.'

In the heyday of the town in the 1950s it was as though nothing could change the euphoric optimism that swept everyone along with it. Miners' wages crept to the top of the earning's ladder – a strong, well led union saw to that. Much of the surplus cash was spent in the splendid shops which lined Station Road, the main street. The five day week meant more leisure time and meant that holidays could now be spent either at home or abroad. How could the good times possibly end? Didn't the experts say that the town was sitting on enough rich seams of coal to last until well past the year 2000? Perhaps they did, but time has proved them wrong. One by one the mines closed because of their high production costs. Some of them – Ashington included – were kept open artificially, although running at a loss. The argument in favour of this being: how can you evaluate the loss of a man's job and, with it, his dignity and the effect upon the community?

Now, with the millennium almost upon us, what of the town of Ashington and its people? Will it stagnate or continue to grow? Where will the youth of tomorrow find jobs? How can things be made better? These are the questions being asked. Whatever the vagaries of tomorrow, the reader of today can now look back, through words and pictures, at the way it was in the 'good owld days'.

Mike Kirkup
February 1999

One

Old Ashington

Inevitably, much of what constituted the Ashington of the past is gone, demolished in the name of progress, and now sorely missed. How often do we hear: 'What did they have to knock that down for? It was a lovely building.' Ashington Boer War Memorial (from around 1910) listed the names of local men who were killed in South Africa. It contained a drinking fountain – ideal for the young children running out of St Aidan's school in the afternoon. Note there is no Council Chambers at the top left, that came a few years later.

The Revd John Bunker had a grisly task when Ashington's first churchyard, attached to the Holy Sepulchre, went up in flames and headstones fell all around him. Was eternal damnation being visited on the coal town back in the 1970s? No, it was all put down to internal combustion, the graveyard being right above some old mine workings.

Woodhorn church, 1890. This is one of the rare photographs which shows the mill with its sails intact. The church dates back to Anglo Saxon times and is now a museum.

Cook's Corner, *c.* 1920. Russell Cook was an influential figure in the early history of Ashington. His department store dominated this corner. Additionally, Stanley Cook owned a shop nearby on North Seaton Road, which sold pet food among other items.

Grand Hotel, *c.* 1930. Built around 1890, the Grand was a magnificent building with fine stained glass windows. It was the first of three public houses built in Ashington after the town went from being a 'dry', liquor-free area to the other end of the scale where it was to be described in 1952 as 'Satan's Citadel' because of its twenty workingmen's clubs. The hotel was demolished in 1983.

Grand Corner, *c.* 1900. 'I will see you at the Grand Corner,' was a favourite saying when arranging to meet up with someone in town. Note that Arrowsmith's has not yet appeared on the left, at this time there are only wooden railings and a path through some bushes.

Station Road, from Station Bridge, *c.* 1920. 'Over the bridge' shopping has always taken place in this quiet part of town.

Stakeford Bridge, 1909. This was the first road bridge to ford the River Wansbeck at this point. It derives its name from stakes along the river bank which measured the tides. When at its lowest, people were able to ford the river to the other side. In the background is the wooden railway bridge built in the 1850s.

The Black Bridge, 1929. This once transported wagons carrying millions of tons of high-class coal from Ashington Coal Company's five pits. In 1999 only Ellington Pit remains.

Station Road, Ashington.

Station Road, looking west, in 1910. The buildings on the left are the Presbyterian church, the police station, St Aidan's Catholic church and the Miners Theatre.

Initially, the railway station was called Hirst Station when it opened in the 1870s. The rail link to Newcastle was severed during the Beeching cuts of 1964, but the line still carries coal from Ellington Colliery and aluminium from Alcan smelter.

Nixon's farm buildings in the 1920s. This site was later used for the first Ashington bus station, and is now a supermarket. Just visible on the left is the Wallaw Cinema.

High Market, looking east, in 1910. The building on the immediate left is the Ashington & District (West End) Social Club.

Station Road, *c.* 1890. There are no shops at all on the left hand side, only a rail track for coal bogies. The path to the railway station, which bisected Ashington and Hirst, is on the right.

Station Road, beside 7th Row, *c.* 1910. There was always a scattering of shops on this stretch of road, plus a Methodist chapel which later became a Salvation Army Hall.

16

Bothal Village, *c. 1920*. This pretty village with its castle and stepping stones over the river, was a favourite haunt of walkers on a Sunday afternoon.

Duke of Portland, 1914. The duke, one of the Bentinck family, who lived in Bothal Castle, owed much of his wealth to the royalties he received by means of the coal extracted from under his land. The duke, William Bentinck, was married in 1893 and had two children. To celebrate his son's birthday on 16 March 1914, he held a sports day in the castle grounds and invited local children to take part. Each child was presented with a medallion engraved: 'William Arthur Henry Bentinck, Marquis of Titchfield'.

Council Chambers, 1912. This was the first permanent home for Ashington Urban District Council. In later years the cupola was removed and the clock was placed in its present location so that it was in a better position to be seen in town.

Hugh Cairns VC, 1918. This is Ashington's only holder of the Victoria Cross. His citation reads: 'For most conspicuous bravery before Valenciennes on first of November, 1918, when a machine gun opened on his platoon...Sergeant Cairns seized a Lewis gun and single handed, in the face of direct fire, rushed the post and captured the gun...although wounded, he showed the highest degree of valour...he died from his wounds on the second of November, 1918.'

Ashington Hospital, 1916. Building began in 1914, but because of the First World War was not completed until two years later. The first patients were wounded soldiers.

Sister Dixon, hospital stalwart, c. 1950. Initial costs for the hospital were borne by Ashington Coal Company who hired Scotsman Frank Gairdner as the first surgeon and built a house for him, 'Ochterlony', at the end of Green Lane. Financing the hospital was then passed on to the miners themselves who had one penny per week levied from their wages. To augment this, many hospital carnivals were held as fundraising events. Sister Dixon became one of the best known of the nursing staff and served in the hospital for many years.

Woodhorn Road showing Wesleyan Lesser Hall in 1900. Methodism in Ashington was always strong. Next door was Humphrey's hardware shop.

Woodhorn Road in the 1960s. Now we see the road much as readers will remember it. The Hirst East End Club is on the left, next to the old Northern Club. In fact at one time there were no fewer than five workingmen's clubs almost next door to each other. The imposing Central Hall is at the end of the road.

Central Hall, Ashington.   66689

Methodist Central Hall was built onto Lesser Hall in 1924 and became the main concert venue for the town. Celebrity concerts arranged by Normanton Barron drew world class musicians and singers (see page 46).

In one moment of madness, in 1989, the Central Hall was demolished, robbing the community of a cultural centre which has yet to be replaced.

Hawthorn Road before and after renovation, 1934. Initially it had been called Humber Terrace, but, like other Ashington streets in this area, the rivers gave way to trees in 1911. So Severn Street became Sycamore and Clyde Street was renamed Chestnut and so on. Before this road was resurfaced it proved to be a nightmare for vehicles.

Malcolm Smith (right) in the 1930s. He appreciated the better roads, driving, as he did, the solid-wheeled coaches of the time from Ashington to Lynemouth.

22

Ashington Co-op joiners in the Store Yard, 1930s. From left to right: W. Baker, John Grenfell, J. Stainsbury, Tom Grenfell, J. Barker, C. Mallaby, G. Chapman, George Brown.

Ashington Co-op Dairy workers, 1940s. Included among those pictured are Billy Lyons (middle row, second from the left), Neville Black (middle row, fifth from the left), Geordie Roy and Cyril Butters (both on the left of the back row).

Jack and Lizzie Kirkup, at the back-end of their house at 187 Chestnut Street in the Hirst, in 1956. Jack Kirkup was one of many who emigrated following the disastrous coal stoppage of 1926. However, disheartened by the fierce Canadian winters, he returned and met and married Lizzie Talbot, one of a family of eleven children, who lived in Sycamore Street.

Wheatley's the butchers, in the 1950s. Horse and cart was the mode of transport used extensively to deliver produce to the colliery rows, as seen here at the 'top-end' of Ashington.

Two

Shops

STATION ROAD END. HIRST, ASHINGTON. 1790.

Station Road ends and Woodhorn Road begins, *c.* 1910. The main street, as it was always called, evolved over a number of years, shops being added piecemeal until retail outlets ranged over the full length of Station Road and beyond. The traffic was light enough for men to conduct their crack in the middle of the road. Brough's grocery store, with cupola, is on the corner, next to the Linton and Woodhorn Miners' Hall, which now houses TSB. Blinds were drawn constantly on that side of the street to protect goods from the sun. Did that heavenly being only shine brightly in the past?

An artist's propaganda impression of what might have happened if Ashington's main street had been bombed by zepellins and invaded during the First World War.

The Grand corner, 1900. Russell Cook's department store is on the left, with George Arrowsmith's shop opposite. These were two of the most upmarket shops in turn of the century Ashington.

Station Road, *c.* 1920. Now there are United buses to contend with on this busy corner. Initially many accidents occurred before people came to terms with this modern mode of transport.

Bertha Lewis and her mother supplied the women of Ashington with their corsets and underwear for over fifty years. They were the sole agents in the town for Spirella corsets. Bertha is seen here in her tiny shop opposite the bus station in the 1970s.

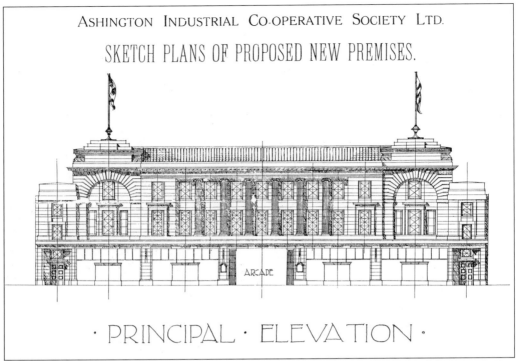

ASHINGTON INDUSTRIAL CO-OPERATIVE SOCIETY LTD.

SKETCH PLANS OF PROPOSED NEW PREMISES.

ARCADE

· PRINCIPAL · ELEVATION ·

Plans for Co-operative Arcade, 1924. This became the jewel in the crown of the town's Co-operative movement, providing employment for Ashington's growing workforce. The best jobs, even at the Co-op, always went to the male of the species, no matter what qualifications were held by girls.

The store Arcade in the 1930s. The Arcade vied with the most elegant department stores in Ashington, providing high class goods at low prices, plus a yearly dividend.

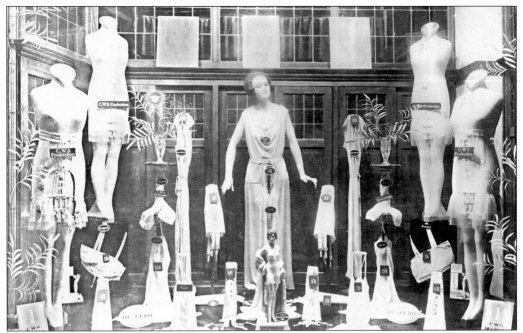

Lingerie department at the Arcade, in the 1930s. This is what the fashion-conscious miner's wife wore under her pinnie.

Ashington Co-op on Woodhorn Road, 1910. Here there were departments for furniture, grocery and meat, among others, all delivered free of charge using the society's own horses.

Stag and Ned Taylor, in the 1930s. Ned (left) was head horse keeper for the Coal Company; he and the impressive shire, Stag, won most of the prizes at local shows.

Co-op on Milburn Road, 1910. When it opened in 1900 this was a branch of the Newbiggin store. Co-op stores were soon to be found all over Ashington, quickly proving to be the most popular shops in town.

Staff at Seaton Hirst Co-op on Hawthorn Road, 1932. In the heyday of co-operative trading, Ashington boasted no fewer than eight stores. John Craigs was the first manager of the Ashington Pit Co-operative, while James Drysdale held a similar position with the Old Pit Co-op. A merger produced the store now in Woodhorn Road. Pictured are some of the staff who worked at the Hawthorn Road branch. From left to right: Sally McElleenan, Billy Gray, Lena Shovelton, Albert Foreman, Albert Mitcheson, Olive Curtis, Bill Benns, Mr Keeble, Olive Evans, with Jackie Wright at the front. Billy Gray was one of four musical brothers who made up part of the Arcadians Dance Band (see page 85). Sadly, Billy was killed while serving in the Royal Air Force during the Second World War.

Blacklock's department store, 1920s. This was a fabulous emporium which added a new dimension to the town's main shopping street. It boasted a café with waitress service and an open-air dance floor on the roof. It was later taken over by Doggarts, and is now Mackays.

Station Road, 1930. By now the main street was settling into a pattern of trading that was to last well into the 1950s. United buses picked up passengers here.

Jimmy Main's bike shop in Laburnum Terrace, 1950. Jimmy was a respected businessman, Rotarian and practical joker. He built a life-size robot in the 1960s, which marched up and down Station Road talking to people. It transpired that Jimmy was hidden inside the robot.

James Chrisp's shop in the 1950s. Jimmy's son-in-law, Ernie Riddle, is seen demonstrating a train set at a Christmas bazaar for the Prior family.

Jackie Milburn's fireplace shop 'over the bridge', in 1953. One of the football legend's many business ventures during his career at Newcastle United.

Giovanni Rossi and his wife, outside their ice-cream and confectionery shop near Pavilion Theatre, in the 1930s. Rossi was one of many Italians who opened shops in the town. (See page 85.)

The 'main street' in 1972. The town centre was still thriving with many of the old shops doing quite well, but change was on the way.

Station Bridge was the first to be dismantled in 1973, when Wansbeck Square was born. The Co-op Dairy (top left) is now a pub called the Black Diamond.

Arrowsmith's department store had one of the town's finest Christmas bazaars. Look at this array of old-fashioned toys. What child could resist the temptation to view the goodies on show? What wonder there was in their eyes as they came up to Santa Claus, face to face. Santa, here in the early 1950s, was played by Alf Whitcombe, sometimes known as Ashington's Mr Charity for the good deeds he carried out in his lifetime. Alf was a staunch member of the Salvation Army.

Ashington's Station Road, 1996. Now pedestrianized, the old street regularly plays host to fairs and band contests. Local celebrity, Sir John Hall, said: 'When I came to build the Metro Centre, I based it on Ashington's main street with a roof on – it was where you met everyone.' Fashions have changed, as long dresses and balaclavas have given way to shell suits and baseball caps; horse and carts have made room for taxis; and good old-fashioned shops, no doubt feeling their age, disappeared from the scene to be replaced by those of a charitable nature.

Three
Entertainment

Miners were traditionally musical. There was something about the brutality of pitwork that steered the pitman towards the harmonious, whether it be singing or playing. This is the Harmonic Band outing, in 1920. An orchestra was formed around 1890 to perform in the Harmonic Hall. Prominent members included Harry Boutland, conductor (with cane) and William Henderson who taught violin. Charabanc trips were often arranged to various Northumberland villages such as Rothbury.

The Harmonic boasted a number of ensembles such as a brass band and full orchestra. Bill Henderson encouraged schoolchildren to play by lending them instruments. Back left in this sextet is Matty Clarke, front left is Tom Allison, with Harry Boutland (front, centre) and Alec Todd (front right).

Miners loved to sing, sometimes just to entertain themselves down the pit. On occasion they formed themselves into Gleemen and visited one of the many clubs in Ashington where they put on a show for an audience. The Wansbeck Gleemen pictured here are, from left to right: Ernie Hamilton, Hennor Wanless, George Turnbull (choirmaster), Dick Barnfather.

Princess Ballroom, *c.* 1936. The Princess began its life as a skating rink, but was soon established as the premier dance hall in town. It was situated just behind the Wallaw cinema, and, from the outside, looked drab. Just step inside though and you were transported into a fantasy world of fairy lights and luxurious fittings, plus a sprung marquet floor on which you could waltz into your own private dream. Sometimes the rink would be booked for a special occasion such as a Police Ball or Rotary Dance. Then the men wore dress suits and bow ties, while the women sparkled in their evening gowns. James Chrisp, seen in the centre at the back, was the owner of one of Ashington's finest shops.

Disaster at the Princess, 4 April 1944. It was a date etched into the minds of thousands of Ashington lads and lasses as their dream went up in smoke, leaving a tangled web of metal as the sole reminder of happy days gone by. A fire broke out inside the dance hall in the small hours of the morning, and by the time it was spotted it was too late – the Princess was gone, never to be replaced. Alf Shepherd, the owner, used the insurance money to buy Newcastle's Oxford Galleries and Old Assembly Rooms.

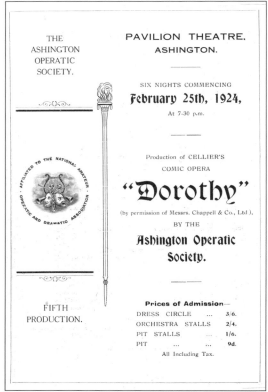

Ashington Thespians Dramatic Society, 1927. For a mining town, Ashington was well served on the cultural side, with no fewer than two operatic societies and numerous amateur dramatic groups. *Lord Richard in the Pantry*, performed at the Miners Theatre, on 24 March 1927, featured William Nixon Craigs, Ailsa Longridge, Fred Thompson, Barbara Beaton, Frank Graham, Edmund Glass, Grace Eskdale, Mrs T. Crozier, Robina Cessford, Lilian Carse, Ethel M. Youngs and Walter Turner.

Programme for Ashington Operatic Society, 1924. The idea that a mining community could sustain its own operatic society was raised when a group of locals attended a concert at Amble in 1919. One of them, music shop owner Benny Creigh, persuaded the Amble director, David Kennedy, to put an Ashington show 'on the boards'. So, *HMS Pinafore* was performed in 1920, the first in a long line of productions which sees Ashington Operatic Society in 1999 still playing to packed audiences.

The Miners Theatre, *c.* 1900. Built originally as a meeting place for miners employed by ACC, the 'Miners', as it became known, went on to play host to itinerant players and musicians, as well as home-grown talent. It became the Regal Cinema in the late 1930s.

The Pavilion Theatre, *c.* 1900. The 'Piv' put on animal acts and plays before going on to show silent movies. Louis Stoddart played piano before talkies arrived – he later managed the cinema. Of five cinemas it is the only one left standing, though it is now a Bingo Hall.

The Hippodrome Theatre stood on Newbiggin Road. It was first owned by Mr Henderson, a caring individual who also opened an institute for the old men of Seaton Hirst. Like the other Ashington theatres, it was eventually taken over by film magnate, Walter Lawson, who gave his name to yet one more picture house.

In the heyday of the cinema, after the Second World War, the town's picture palaces, combined, could cater for 4,200 people at one sitting. It was possible to see a film in the first house at the Regal (Miners) and race a couple of hundred yards down Station Road to catch the second house at the Buffalo. On Sunday night each cinema, apart from the 'Hipp', showed the same movie; a young lad was employed to take the film, reel by reel, on his bike, to the next cinema. Punctures were not allowed!

Normanton Barron, without doubt, was responsible for bringing the best that was around in music to Ashington. He organized his own choirs and orchestras as well as bringing the cream of international talent to the town. Kathleen Ferrier, Joan Hammond and the Polish singer Nowakwski, all played at the Central Hall in Norman's time.

Wallaw Cinema ends with *Annie*, in August 1982. It was a sad day for the town when the last of its cinemas closed. Television had changed the habits of a lifetime and people simply stopped coming through the doors. On hand to bid a fond farewell was the last projectionist Denis Cleugh, manager Jean Herron and a clutch of faithful staff.

The Princess Ballroom Band Wedding, in the 1930s. A 'reet' grand affair as Ronnie Hope and his young bride-to-be were marched musically down Bothal Bank to the church. Princess owner Alf Shepherd is on left, popular musician Harry Hoggarth is on the right, playing the cymbals.

Arcadians Dance Band, 1948. The Gray brothers brought pleasure to thousands of young Ashington folk. They enlisted good musicians like Jimmy Locker, Jim Hunt, Malcolm McKenzie and Les Stevenson plus many others, while singers Eric Nichol and Connie Allsopp (both featured above) combined to bring the authentic big band sound to the mining community.

The Arcade Hall was probably the best loved of all the town's dancehalls once the Rink had burned down. It opened in the mid-1920s, initially as a meeting hall for lectures on the Co-operative movement. Would-be employees also took their entrance exams here.

BBC Television featured some of Ashington's top talent in 1956, including The Five Beaux and a Belle which consisted of Bill Jordan, Eric Nichol, Doris Pearson, Ben Cherrington, Dickie Slaughter and Alan Richardson; a former Belle was Lillian Browell.

The Wesleyan Central Hall was fortunate in 1963 to acquire the services of Sheila Armstrong to head one of their Sunday night celebrity concerts. Also on the bill that night was Bedlington born violinist Kenneth Sillito and the Choral Union Choir.

The Central Hall Orchestra, organized and conducted by Normanton Barron, featured the cream of the area's musicians. During the Second World War, small ensembles played for troops stationed in Northumberland.

Local songwriting duo Derek Hobbs and Mike Kirkup staged their first musical in 1975. Entitled *Song of the Coal*, it featured the teaching staff of Ashington High School. Pictured here are: Sue Garrett, Iris Penny, Gwen Nicholson, Jean Paul, Gwen Woodman, Barbara Keating, Barbara Wells and Sue Greenwood.

Song of the Coal depicted one day in the life of a set of fillers down the pit and their bickering wives in the back street. 'Do you know what her nickname is, lasses? Tin-opener Trixie! They reckon there is more scrap tin lying at the back of her house than there is at Rammy's Ranch.'

The same composer and writer (pictured above) teamed up again to write the musical *Fell 'em Doon* in 1994 which told the story of the birth of the pit village. As well as soprano Maureen Williams, seen here with the writers, other main parts were taken by Tim Jones and Gillian Ramshaw.

Fell 'em Doon was a massive community effort featuring over 300 children from 11 local schools as well as an adult choir of 120 and massed brass bands. Some of the children from Moorside First School are seen at one of the rehearsals.

Four

Education

The first school to be built in Ashington was in the High Market area. Ashington then was still deemed a village in the parish of Bothal, so Bothal School was the name it took on opening in 1873. One of the first teachers, Miss Joisce, found that the girls had been mechanically coached into practically every movement they made in class. On the command 'stand', they went through a complicated drill of turning and putting the right hand on the desk behind them, swinging both legs over the seat to the other side, standing up, facing the front. On the command 'sit', they performed the whole thing in reverse. Pictured above, from left to right, front row: -?-, Norah Robinson, Nellie Cooper, Barbara Makepeace (with slate) Zipra Wilson, Ethel Wardle, -?-. Second row: Ethel Riddell, Nancy Ritson, Nellie Floyd, Meggie Davison, Annie Thompson, Meggie Riddell. Third row: -?-, -?-, Daisy Anderson, Meggie Dixon, Nellie Keeble, ? Arkle. Back row: ? Davison, ? Fitzpatrick, ? Atkinson, Dolly Atkinson, ? Willis, Meggie Johnson, Miss Shell (teacher).

The Hirst North School was the next to be built, in 1896, to cater for miners' children in the Hirst part of town. It was a massive building catering for upwards of 1,500 children. Working as a well drilled team was an educational demand placed upon the pupils in the early days. A strict regime meant that few pupils were disruptive. Miss Joisce, a teacher at Bothal School said, 'One day a girl called Lena Ward gave me a parcel, saying that it was a present from her father. Inside was a leather taws with my initials, SJ, cut in the top. The girl's father was a saddler at the colliery. This was his way of saying "Use it with my blessing".'

Boys and girls from the North School were entered each year in various county competitions, either for singing, dance, drama or choric speech. The four girls who won the Dicken's Banner in the 1930s; Molly Weightman, Audrey Nesbitt, Audrey Stimpson and Mary Laing, all went on to have distinguished careers.

Ashington pupils were entered in competitions run by various bodies such as the North of England Music Festival. This ensemble from Hirst North Junior Girls Dramatic Society won the Besley Challenge Trophy for *In Goblin Glen*, a play they performed in the 1936 Whitley Bay Dramatic Festival.

Many of the female teachers at Hirst North were held in great affection by the girls. Miss Vida Sample (at the back, second from the left) with over forty years of service was the North School's longest serving teacher. From left to right, back row: Cissie Greenan, Vida Sample, Ethel Kirsopp, Margaret Richardson, Grace Clark, Mary Bruce. Front row: Connie Hall, Dora Besford, Isabel Smith (headteacher), Connie Dent, Marjorie Webster.

After providing education for 101 years, the North School (uppies and doonies) was finally demolished in 1997 and the remaining 400 children were transferred just over the road to the New North School. The school has since been renamed.

In a reunion of past pupils to mark its centenary, three of the young award winners (see page 50) came back to say farewell to the old school: Mary Armstrong (née Laing), Miss Audrey Stimpson and Audrey Pyle (née Nesbitt).

One of Ashington's oldest schools was St Aidan's, built in 1894, opposite the police station. The schoolyard was split into girls (on the near side) and boys, by a long brick wall. When the boys played football at break-times, the ball invariably ended up in the priest's garden in front of the presbytery (top left).

Headmaster during the 1930s and '40s was Mr Michael McGough, pictured on the left. The Catholic children were honour bound to go to Mass every Sunday, which was also attended by the headmaster. Some wag composed this verse: 'Mr McGough has a bad cough, he goes to church on Sundays. He prays to God to give him strength to whack us kids on Mondays.'

SOUTH SCHOOLS, HIRST, ASHINGTON. 1793.

After the North School was built, the population of the Hirst part of town grew so much that they built another school, rather unimaginatively called the South School.

Pupils who played for the South School football team in 1954 welcomed back an old boy, Ron Routledge, who was then playing goalkeeper for Sunderland. The lad sitting on the far left, John Ritchie, later played league football for the team managed by Stanley Matthews.

54

With schools for the North and the South, it was inevitable that the next school to be built in 1913 would be called the East School. A mixed school, East catered for infants who lived geographically to the east of Hawthorn Road. Pupils then went to North School when aged 9 and came back to East to complete their secondary education at the age of 11 plus. By then the more academic pupils would have passed their scholarship and gone on to grammar schools at Morpeth or Bedlington, although a 13 plus exam at East School invariably found late starters who blossomed there and went on to distinguish themselves at Blyth Grammar School. East is now called Alexandra Middle School.

Logically, the next school to be built in Ashington should have been called the West. In fact it was the Central School, built in 1928 beside a large ash tip on the corner of 3rd Avenue and Hawthorn Road. When the ashes were cleared in the 1930s, grass seeds were sown which flourished and produced a wonderful expanse of green field, a veritable park, in fact.

From that day on, the latest Ashington education establishment became known as the Hirst Park Modern School. Still retaining its name today in spite of being a Middle School, one of the Park's best-known pupils, apart from footballer Jack Charlton, was opera singer Sheila Armstrong, seen standing on the right at a school presentation. As a 13-year-old schoolgirl, Sheila was hailed as England's own Judy Garland, after a stunning performance on BBC television as part of Ashington's Top Town Team.

All children love a party, especially if it is held outdoors. This bash was in Hawthorn Road to celebrate the coronation of King George VI in 1937. Young Frankie Preston (third from the right) looks eager to get on with it.

Traditional games were on the curriculum when the Wansbeck School opened in 1932 next to the Holy Sepulchre church. Apart from wheeling steel hoops (called gords), there were the usual skipping games, two-ball piny against the wall (mostly for girls), and the physical challenge of 'mount the cuddy' with the object being to mount as many bodies as possible on to a two-man cuddy (a mule) crouched against the wall.

The young lads of Ashington often formed themselves into street gangs. Not the kind of gangs that would create any trouble, just a friendly coming together of young miners. This one in Ariel Street is an example. Back row, from left to right: Dick Morton, Alan Fenwick, Jimmy Keegan, Stan Fenwick, Billy Partis, Arthur Charlton, John Jacques. In the centre is Bob Morton. Front row: Dickie Partis and son, John Thompson, John 'Cocky' Wren, Jack Moreton, Doug Yeowart. It was obvious that someone on the local council had a wry sense of humour when he named the streets in the Hirst part of town. Having given the first eleven colliery rows only numbers, 1st Row, 2nd Row and so on, he then went over the top and called streets after Shakespearian characters like Rosalind, Juliet and Portia. In spite of living in Ariel Street in the 1940s, there was nothing fairy-like about this bunch of lads!

Of course the youth of Ashington could join any number of organizations specially designed for the younger element of the town. One such organization was the Co-operative Youth Club, seen here in 1942 with some of their members serving in the forces. Bill Williams is in the middle row, second from the left. Others pictured include Colin McNiven, Peggy White, Mary Dobson (Jack's daughter) and Vera Purdy. Reporter/organizer Alan Robson (wearing glasses) sits at the front, in the centre.

The first school which catered for mining students was simply formed by knocking two houses together near the pit. Custom-built in 1930, the Mining School in Darnley Road was originally intended to nurture the young talented lads of the area who wanted to make a full-time career in the coal industry. Many of them became officials in other collieries; such as this group in 1942. From left to right, back row: Mr Richell (caretaker), Cecil Bennett, Gabriel Burns, Jimmy Muir, Bill Williams, George Strong, Jimmy Scott, Bill Douglas, Johnnie Burton, Tommy Bland. Sitting: Herby Young Robinson, Mr R.L. Hay, Donald Hindson (agent), Mr Frank Graham, Mr Lowe.

The Mining School became the focal point for many other organizations, such as the Air Training Corps who, in the 1940s, provided the RAF with eager young men, fully trained in all aspects of the war. Back row, from left to right: K. Shaw, E. Arkle, Don Turner, E.J. Bell, Bill Kennedy. Front row: J. Dawson, J. Baird, George Strong, Ray Bowart, R. Morris.

This gang of ATC lads, nicknamed the 'Winnie Bush Bombers', chose to go on a working holiday to a farm near Belford in the early '40s. Included among those pictured, on the back row are: Mr Richell, Les Agan, George Rogerson, Ron Coulson, Jim Harle, Jackie Milburn, Jackie Gray. Middle row: Bob Kennedy and the son of Donald Hindson. Front row: Alan Bell, Cecil Straker, Joe Lawson, Ned Arkle, Fred Weddell. Norman Brotherton took the photograph.

Welfare grounds were set up at each of the pit villages, catering for girls as well as boys. Ashington Rec, with its backdrop of pit heaps and railway trucks was the venue for many sports including tennis. The ladies pictured are, from left to right, back row: Mrs Beal (née Curry), Margaret Richardson, Miss Aitcheson (the stationmaster's daughter). Front row: Noreen Hedley (née Nixon), Peggy Jamieson, Winnie Barron (née Garvie). The Rec was built on waste ground in the 1880s and became popular with the sports-minded mining community. A cycle track was formed around the playing fields and it soon catered for races of up to one hundred miles. The fully equipped gymnasium was used by hundreds of would-be gymnasts and boxers. Table tennis enthusiasts began their own league and often invited top professionals such as Victor Barna to play exhibition matches.

Hirst Welfare was priceless to the Ashington Coal Company and its men. Bought from Milburn Estates for only thirty-two shillings an acre, it claimed to have some of the best sporting facilities for miles around. Apart from the seven football pitches, there were tennis courts, cricket and hockey pitches, a running track, a gym which doubled as dance hall, and a six-table billiard hall. It was also the venue for children's galas once a year, and outdoor country dancing – seen here in 1947 with Woodhorn pit heaps and chimney in the background. The No. One football pitch was arguably the best in the county. Now, in 1999, the Welfare lies derelict, and plans to move Ashington FC to the site have not as yet materialized.

Ashington Swimming Baths opened in 1932. The miners were given the choice of having pit-head baths, but opted instead for the swimming baths, saying that it was up to the Coal Company to provide indoor baths in the colliery houses. In fact, it was not until 1952 that Ashington miners had their own pit-head baths (see page 125). Here we see a victorious Ashington YMCA team around 1950.

Two famous Ashington faces and one not so familiar. There were four Charlton brothers, but only two, Jack on the left and Bobby on the right, were in the limelight. Their brothers Gordon (centre) and Tommy continued careers outside football.

Jack and Bobby Charlton became international figures overnight in July 1966 as the first brothers to play for England in a successful World Cup Final. They are completely different characters: Jack is the more forthright, volatile yet warm-hearted; Sir Bobby is the quiet one, content, in his playing days, to let his shooting boots do the talking. The latter is not as likely now, as his outspoken brother, to recognise the Charlton family roots in the clarty back streets of yesteryear Ashington. They are seen here in 1966 outside Bothal Castle.

Going to a Catholic school in 1950 at St Aidan's meant that you had to attend your First Communion at around seven years of age. Boys were dressed in new clothes, a white shirt and red tie. Girls wore white dresses – sometimes their mother's cut-down wedding dress and veil. Both sexes wore white sandshoes. The well loved teacher is Miss Hannah Bell.

The coronation of Queen Elizabeth II in 1953 was celebrated in Ashington with a big bonfire in Peoples Park. Vince Gledhill (wearing glasses) is seen with John Forster and two sisters, Marlene and Celia Weatherall, all from the Alexandra Road/Ariel Street vicinity.

Ashington Grammar School opened in 1959 to a fanfare of acclaim. The first headmaster was George Chapman, second from the left, with governors Norman Brotherton and Cllr James Tilley, and a local vicar.

Ashington's County Technical College was an offshoot of the Mining School, catering initially for mining and engineering students. It opened in 1956 and in those days was only three storeys high, it has since grown to six storeys.

A pupil from Hirst High School, Gene Healey, provided the design for Ashington's newest war memorial, unveiled in 1983. The controversial sculpture by Colin Rose represents three First World War soldiers in gas-capes.

A group of cooks, dinner ladies and assistants from Ashington Grammar School are waited on themselves for a change at the Portland Hotel in the 1960s.

Five
Recreation

Most people in Ashington had some connection with mining, either working at the pit or taking care of those who did. This meant there was little time for relaxation through the week, so weekends were utilized to the full. Playing in a jazz band was one way of ensuring that children didn't get into any mischief. Led by the late 'Tucker' McLeod, Ashington Melody Makers often paraded Station Road during carnivals like this in the 1960s.

Hirst Flower Park, laid out in 1916, was always a favourite haunt of locals on a Sunday afternoon. The statue was erected in memory of thirteen men killed in an explosion at Woodhorn Pit in 1916 (see page 115). It is now situated at Woodhorn Colliery Museum.

Hirst Park bowlers were always a successful team. They are represented here by, from left to right, back row: Dick Talbert, -?-, Percy Drew, Harry Saint, Harry Clark, Jim Sinclair, Eddie Simpson, Davey Home, Geordie Taylor, -?-, -?-, ? Henderson, -?-, ? Tullock. Front row: Jack Marshall, Arthur Wright, Jim Forster, Joe Wren, Geordie Middleton.

Larry Bell started up a Boys Club in a shed outside his house in Park View in the 1940s. Soon he had hundreds of members, running four football teams and a boxing squad. Larry is at the back, second from the left.

Ashington had two Motor Clubs in the 1940s. Here Inspector Jim Macintosh, third from the right, checks the contestants before a road safety competition starting from John Buck's garage behind Lintonville Terrace.

Greyhound racing came to Ashington's Portland Park in 1936. It was not welcomed by many religious organizations, but quickly became popular with the miners and their families. Cosa Maite, pictured above, was a 1940 record holder.

976th MEETING

INVEST ON THE "TOTE" EARLY –
DELAY MAY CAUSE DISAPPOINTMENT

ASHINGTON
STADIUM
Dial Ashington 2195

LOST £3

PROGRAMME

WEDNESDAY, OCT. 27th, 1948

NEXT MEETING – SATURDAY, OCT. 30th – 7 p.m.

LATEST TRIALS

395 yds H'cap. 24.12		**395 yds H'cap.** 24.46
General Jack (8yd)		Allen Choice (10yd)
Mollys Dasher (sc) bn hd	**495 yds H'cap.** 28.90	Whitsun Defiance (6) bn hd
Bolacrean Swell (4yd) bn ¾	Jambo (sc) solo	Whitsun Dandy (sc) bn ½
Master Mind (12yd) bn 1		Tally (4yd) bn distance
395 yds H'cap. 23.50	**495 yds H'cap.** 29.68	**395 yds H'cap.** 24.57
Viewmount Again (sc)	Inlers Prince (10yd)	Token (4yd)
Valiant (4yd) bn 3 lths	J..c..ie (4yd) bn head	Boyne Ranger (6yd) bn hd
Farloes Gift (8yd) bn 13 ls	Hazel Jubilee (sc) bn 1¾ ls	Whitsun Duke (sc) bn ½

E. N. Davison (T.U.), Printer, Advertiser Office, Ashington.

Hundreds of pounds were wagered Mondays and Saturdays on either the flickering totalisator or with the string of bookies who frequented the track. Bookmakers such as Charlie Chisholm, Joe Embleton and George Rowell. However, the greyhound fraternity was always at odds with the football club who shared the ground. It all ended acrimoniously in the 1960s when the footballers booted the dogs and their owners into touch.

Growing leeks was always a favourite pastime with miners and, perhaps more unexpectedly, so was the cultivation of gladioli. An expert, the late Ivor Bird, hands over a trophy to John Chrisp and John Baird in 1969 at the Excelsior Club, one of twenty clubs then in Ashington.

Ashington's Children's Gala was an annual event from the year 1900. Each school paraded to Peoples Park (or Hirst Welfare after 1950) to receive some cash and sweets. Here miners' union men, George Nelson (left) and Tommy Davison (right) shepherd the children off First Avenue. The event was discontinued in the 1970s owing to lack of support from teachers.

Ashington YMCA has provided relaxation and sporting facilities for over one hundred years. Initially housed in a wooden hut down the 'Buff' Bank, a new prefabricated building was erected in 1959. Dr Jim Hobbs (far left), as president, was a guest of organizer R.J. Vince and his wife (seated) at the offical opening.

The building came in bits and pieces but was up in place when the Princess Royal arrived to do the honours. The YMCA now plays host to many educational and cultural organizations. The excellent Drama Group, after staging productions for many years, is awaiting an influx of fresh blood. However, the four billiard tables continue to pull in the wannabe Geordie Collins and Bill Shiels of the future.

A victorious YMCA billiard team from 1936, winners of the Francis Priestman trophy. Priestman was the son of the original coalowner Jonathon Priestman, a Quaker from Darlington.

Another excellent billiard squad in the period around the Second World War was the Harmonic, playing in the hall opposite the police station. Their team is standing at the back with cues, from left to right: J.W. Lillico, Jack Smith, Bob Barass, ? Hedley. The identity of the other team is unknown.

Priestman's Institute on North Seaton Road was built long before the council put a proper road outside. It had a library and reading room with every daily newspaper. A large games room catered for darts, dominoes, draughts and cards.

There were six tables in two rows of three. Number one table was kept almost exclusively for the members of the Priestman billiard team which, in the '40s and '50s included Norman Harrison, Jim Henderson, Billy Buttles and Billy Staines. Mike Kirkup is seen cueing up on number five table in 1956. The lad at the back, to the left, is a Chapman.

The Ashington Group of Painters gained worldwide attention when they began to chart their own history on canvas in the 1930s. Their first meeting place was in the old YMCA building. On the left is George Brown, Jack Harrison is in the centre and Henry Young is on the right; that's Henry's dog, Dot, doing the posing.

Jack Harrison's sketch of his father, Jim, in a typical miner's pose: clay pipe in mouth, midgie lamp hanging from his belt and wearing a pair of hoggers (trousers) cut below the knee. This was the garb of a hewer of coal, a man who hacked away at the hard seam using a sharp pick. Hewers were the best paid men in the mines in the early days, earning their wage by the tonnage of coal they sent to the bank (surface). Miners worked three shifts; foreshift in the middle of the night, backshift from early morning and nightshift – the graveyard shift – from late afternoon until midnight.

To ride a pit pony underground was illegal, but many putters (see page 119) paid little heed to that. Some lucky ponies were brought to the surface during a carnival to race in the Pit Pony Derby in Peoples Park, like this one in 1932.

Carnivals were held in the 1920s and '30s to help pay for the upkeep of Ashington Hospital. Many floats were placed on carts and lorries, each with a separate theme. This parade is coming from the direction of Holy Sepulchre, passing the 8th and 9th Row gardens.

Jimmy Main was a well known bike man in Ashington, with his shop at the top of Laburnum Terrace. He organized a scooter rally in Peoples Park when this make of machine became popular in the early 1960s. The late Bobby Stoker is on left-hand scooter.

Swimming became part of the curriculum for schools in the 1940s. Once a week each Ashington school had an hour in the pool. Here it is the turn of Hirst North Girls. The high board where they are posing was later dismantled because it was thought to be too dangerous.

Miners love to sing, always have done. These members of the YMCA Gleemen in 1949 were no exception. There are still two male voice choirs in the town; the Ashington and the Wansbeck and District.

Scouting has always been popular, with many troops scattered around the town, some affilliated to churches, others non-denominational. Some of the early Scout leaders from the 1920s were Jack Dorgan, Ross and Dick Miles and George Tomlinson. Venues were always a bit spartan, but that did not deter the dedicated Scout. This is the 1st Hirst Troop who won most of the awards that year, around 1938.

A group of St Aidan's parishioners on a day trip in 1950. Father Sheedy, pictured in the background, died not long afterwards.

Let's hope that those day trippers did not have to rely on this bus attempting to get up Bothal Bank in the late '20s. The United Bus Company were then using vehicles which had seen service in the First World War.

Great emphasis was placed on taking care of the retired miner. The Ashington Veteran's Hut, beside the Central Hall, was opened by coalowners and officials in 1932. Those wearing trilbys are gaffers, while those in cloth caps are retired miners.

One of the five cinemas in town was the Buffalo Picture Palace, as seen in the 1930s. Originally owned by the Grand Order of Buffaloes, it was managed by Joe Lamb before being taken over by Walter Lawson's Wallaw Pictures.

In the 1920s, the record player came on to the market. One of the first shops to stock this new-fangled contraption was Len Shearer on Station Bridge who would place a loudspeaker on the pavement, playing the pop records of the day to anyone who was passing. The lady on the right is Helen Hope, later to become the mother of George Elliott, a dedicated Salvationist.

Young girls enjoyed themselves by singing with the Ashington Operatic Society, seen here as Indian squaws in *Rose Marie* at the Pavilion Theatre in 1934. Among the girls pictured are: Gladys Morgan, Jean Pyle, Ena Conway, Olive Dixon, Alison Bell, Hannah Robson, Anna Purdy, Gladys Boutland (at the front, third from the left) and Hilda Allison.

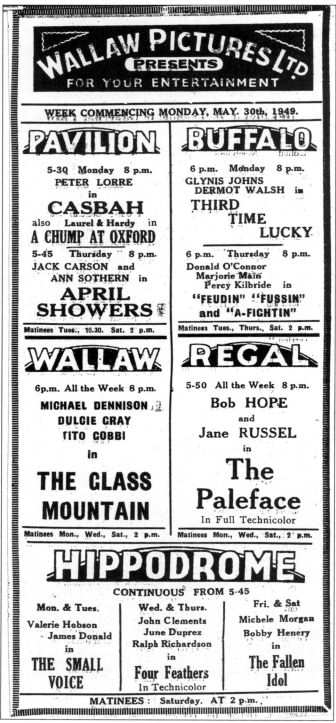

WALLAW PICTURES LTD.

PRESENTS

FOR YOUR ENTERTAINMENT

WEEK COMMENCING MONDAY, MAY. 30th, 1949.

PAVILION

5-30 Monday 8 p.m.
PETER LORRE
in
CASBAH
also Laurel & Hardy in
A CHUMP AT OXFORD

5-45 Thursday 8 p.m.
JACK CARSON and
ANN SOTHERN in
APRIL SHOWERS

Matinees Tues., 10.30. Sat. 2 p.m.

BUFFALO

6 p.m. Monday 8 p.m.
GLYNIS JOHNS
DERMOT WALSH in
THIRD TIME LUCKY

6 p.m. Thursday 8 p.m.
Donald O'Connor
Marjorie Main
Percy Kilbride in
"FEUDIN" "FUSSIN" and "A-FIGHTIN"

Matinees Tues., Thurs., Sat. 2 p.m.

WALLAW

6 p.m. All the Week 8 p.m.
MICHAEL DENNISON
DULCIE GRAY
TITO GOBBI
in
THE GLASS MOUNTAIN

Matinees Mon., Wed., Sat., 2 p.m.

REGAL

5-50 All the Week 8 p.m.
Bob HOPE
and
Jane RUSSEL
in
The Paleface
In Full Technicolor

Matinees Mon., Wed., Sat., 2 p.m.

HIPPODROME

CONTINUOUS FROM 5-45

Mon. & Tues.	Wed. & Thurs.	Fri. & Sat.
Valerie Hobson James Donald in **THE SMALL VOICE**	John Clements June Duprez Ralph Richardson in **Four Feathers** In Technicolor	Michele Morgan Bobby Henery in **The Fallen Idol**

MATINEES : Saturday. AT 2 p.m.

What you could expect to see at one of the five cinemas in May 1949. The cost of admission in the stalls was seven pence with threepence extra to pay if you went upstairs.

ARCADIANS DANCE BAND

JUBILEE
Celebration Ball
May 6th. — 8 p.m. to 1 a.m.

WED. - SAT. NIGHTS

"ARCADE" ASHINGTON

Silver Jubilee

1910-1935

The Arcade Hall was intended to be a meeting place for lectures. Instead it became the hottest place in town – a meeting place for young lovers! Where else could you put your arms around someone of the opposite sex without a word of protest? Twice weekly dances were attended by hundreds – and holy matrimony was only a waltz away.

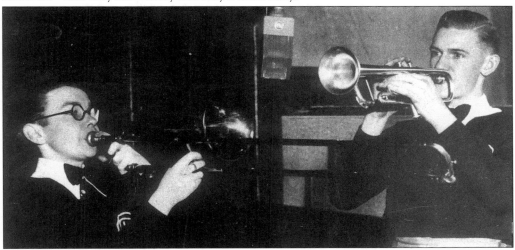

Yet it had been oh, so different, until that fateful date (see page 39). The date that was to ring like a death knell among the young teeny boppers of the day. It was the date the Princess Ballroom burned to the ground. The wonderful Princess. Gone but not forgotten. Certainly not by Billy Mason, still in his teens when playing trombone alongside Ronnie Hope on the trumpet.

A much later hotspot in the 1960s was the Three Ones nightclub, originally the Harmonic Hall. The name came from its address, 111 Station Road. Here you could catch a cabaret featuring those glamorous showgirls, croon along with compère Eric Nichol, and chuck your money away on the roulette wheel with croupier Peter Rossi. What a pity that the joint got raided and had its license withdrawn.

If you wanted to get away from the grime of the Ashington colliery rows, then the place to go was Newbiggin by the Sea. The 1950s was a superb time for this little seaside resort when it was invaded by thousands of tourists at weekends and bank holidays. A favourite ride for children was on a pleasure craft, but the exciting part was waiting on the long ramp which stretched right into the sea.

Photographed among the fallen ladders in the corridor of the Arcade Hall in 1949 was one of many rare talents to come out of Ashington. Accordionist Peter Cosimini once toured and played on radio with Felix Mendelsshon and his Hawaiian Serenaders. Peter who fronted his own band at the Rex Hotel in Whitley Bay, agreed to play at the Arcade in aid of Ashington Football Supporters, whose officials are seen on right with George Cave (third from the right). The Cosimini family was only a small part of the Italian connection with Ashington and district. It all began when young Alfredo Marchetti from the hills of Somocollonia in Tuscany decided to try his hand at opening an ice-cream shop in a north-east boom town called Ashington. He was told that coal had been discovered there, and money was to be made. His first shop in Station Road proved to be so successful that he was able to send for his brother and three friends. Other like-minded Italians followed suit. In turn each of these made good with their own business; Giovanni Rossi, Renato 'Sammy' Badiali, Christopher Arrigi and Renzo and Harry Cosimini, the father of Peter. Renzo had a fish shop beside the Mortimer Club, while Harry's 'plaice' was in Seventh Avenue. Other Italians to settle locally included Mazzolini, Bimbi, Pieroni, Gallone, Notorianni and Jimmy Padretti. The Bertorelli brothers headed for the sunshine at Newbiggin by the Sea to open two cafés, one of which is still there.

The League of Labour Youth
(ASHINGTON BRANCH)

A GRAND
CARNIVAL DANCE
will be held in
THE ARCADE HALL
on Friday, May 6th, 1949

Fancy Hats, Streamers
Confetti and Balloons
Spot Prizes and Novelty Dances

Dancing 8 p.m. till 1 am.
Music by J. Dalkin and His Rhythm Boys
ADMISSION - 3/- EACH

We invite all young people to get their tickets
NOW from Mr. G. Robinson, 2 Holly Street
Ashington or J. Dalkin's Band.

Joe Dalkin and his Rhythm Boys only played at the Arcade on special occasions. You could usually see him at North Seaton Welfare, tickling the ivories with the remaining fingers of his right hand. Normally to be heard at the Arcade Hall was Joe Gray and the Arcadians, fronted by Eric Nichol and the lovely Connie Allsopp.

If writing is your means of relaxation you could do worse than join the Wansbeck Writers every Wednesday morning in the YMCA. It could be you writing the next blockbuster. Some of their members have passed away since this photograph was taken in 1990. Included among those pictured are: Elisabeth Jeffrey (seated second from the left), Hilda Rogers (seated, far right) and Ivy Miley (at the back, fourth from the left).

One local character who took the plunge into print is Bill Kell, seen here signing copies of his *Best Scotch or Ordinary* at St Aidan's Parish Centre in November 1997.

Two ex-pitmen collaborated in 1992 on a book called *Gallowa*, about a pit pony. Mike Kirkup, the author, began to work down the mine on leaving school at fifteen. Jim Slaughter (left), who illustrated the book, was a miner before going into teaching at Seaton Hirst Middle School. They are seen here in a mock-up pit roadway at Woodhorn Colliery Museum. Photograph by Reuben Daglish.

Amusements and children's rides came to Peoples Park at least once a year. They were commonly called 'The Shows'. Jack Nesbitt who later ran the Linton Bus is seen here showing off his horse and cart.

Children were sent to dancing classes run by two local lasses: Molly Metcalfe and Peggy Maxwell, who is seen here with her troupe in the Trade Union Hall in 1950. Among those pictured are: Pauline Richardson, Iris Jenkins, Pat Bowie, Catherine Griffin, Peggy Maxwell, Elizabeth Rogers, Pat Foster, Linda Mavin, Shirley Robinson, Angela Hately, Gail Tanney, Kathleen Brown, Sally Clark, Maureen Griffin, Joyce Taylor, Pat Jamieson, Audrey Moody, Vicki Smith and Elizabeth Surtees.

Ashington YMCA Drama Group always could be guaranteed to put on a good show. None more so than in 1948 with above artistes: Fred Weddell, Albert Warham, Joyce Croft, Bob Jeffreys, Mary Boyd, Vera Allan, Elizabeth Wilson, Jean Foster, Jimmy Middlemiss, Mary Crosby and Leslie Ashman.

And the YMCA were always involved in supporting local carnivals, as seen in Peoples Park in 1960.

Six

Sport

In the coal town of Ashington, there were only two choices open to young lads on leaving school – go down the pit or earn a living by playing football. Only a few managed the latter. So football fans from Ashington had a special reason for being in London for the 1951 FA Cup Final. Not only was Newcastle United in the Final, but the town's special son, Jackie Milburn, was playing for the Magpies. Wor Jackie went on to score both goals in their 2-0 defeat of Blackpool. Pictured on the right is colliery engineer, Jack Leithead who married Milburn's sister Jean, with Malcolm Smith who was initially a bus driver then a NCB driver, Harry White who worked in the brickyard, and Jack Davison a driver for County Buses and Gordon's of Stakeford.

The town was also good at turning out great goalkeepers. Seen here at a charity game at Hirst Welfare are Billy Down and Jimmy Potts who played for Burnley and Leeds, respectively. Billy was the father of the Down boys who all played local football. Jimmy was part of the Milburn era at Leeds United in the 1930s, having married into the family.

Here is the Milburn clan in the 1950s, from left to right: George, Jack, Jim, Stan and Jackie Milburn with Bob and Cissie Charlton (née Milburn), parents of Jack and Bobby Charlton (who are seated on the right).

It was Jackie Milburn who put the town of Ashington on the map with his goal scoring exploits for Newcastle United and England. When he stopped playing in the late 1950s, the mantle fell upon the two Charlton brothers. Jackie is seen here at Newcastle Central railway station with his cousin Cissie Charlton and celebrity broadcaster and MP, Clement Freud.

Jackie Milburn began his footballing career at Hirst East School under the watchful eye of Mr Jack Denton, the headmaster. Jackie is seated second from the right with his schoolfriends of 1936.

If you could play football, you could run. If proof were needed of that you could always point at Eddie Poxton, Harry Harle and George Dusty Down. The trio played at all levels, but what made them unique was that they were the only Ashington men to win gold medals at the Scottish Powderhall Meeting which took place for professional sprinters every New Year's Day. They are seen here together at Woodhorn Colliery Museum in 1996. Photograph by Mike Parker.

Professional running was great because you didn't need to be the fastest man in the world to enjoy it. Meetings took place most Saturdays in the summer. This one was in Hirst Park in 1949 and shows Billy Lyons (W. Weaver) second from the left, winning a cross-tie from George Copper Reed on the left, and Tweddle and Ventners.

Foot Handicaps always coincided with Flower Shows. Each colliery town and village staged their own show on the same Saturday each year. For Ashington it was the second Saturday in August, as seen in this 1938 programme. The Lyons bothers, Tommy and Charlie, took charge of the proceedings.

ASHINGTON, HIRST AND BOTHAL HORTICULTURAL SOCIETY

56th ANNUAL EXHIBITION
WILL BE HELD IN THE

Peoples Park, Ashington

SATURDAY, AUG. 13th 1938

£35 - 100 YARDS FOOT HANDICAP

1st Prize £26 and Gold Medal together with Silver Cup to be held for 12 months

2nd £3   3rd 10/-   4th 5/-   5th 5/-
£5 will be divided among Heat Winners who do not compete in the Final.

Handicapper & Judge........ T. LYONS, Ashington
Starter...........................C. LYONS, Ashington
Caller...........................T. CLOUGH, Ashington

RULES

Any runner going over his mark, either hands or feet, will be Penalised ½ yd the 1st offence. 1 yd the 2nd offence [1½ in all] 3rd time disqualified.
All boys must be under 18 years of age and must be able to produce their birth certificate when asked.
Runners entering for the first time must state their last three performances also their addresses for the last 2 years.
Any runner who enters to try to mislead the Handicapper will be immediately disqualified and counted as a runner.
All runners on entering place themselves at the discretion of the Handicapper and his decision is final.
All runners entering for the first time, must state their proper name along with their running name.

Admission 1/-   Programmes 3d
Bookmakers Stands 4/- Including Callers Fee

OPEN DART COMPETITION.   QUOITS.
Ankle Competition (Ladies). ALSATION DOG DISPLAY

Secretary : Mr J. Grieve, 21 Sixth Row, Ashington

If you didn't run in the summer then chances are that you played cricket. If you mention cricket in Ashington then you have to include Stan Levison. Stan has served the Langwell Crescent team, man and boy – taking over as umpire in 1966 when he put away his trusty bat. He is seen here in November 1965 with his wife Mary, after being presented with an engraved tea service.

The Ashington cricket team has represented the town for over one hundred years, playing initially at the Rec before moving to its present home at Langwell Crescent. The team has not always been successful, either on the pitch or off it. They have often looked to local benefactors such as bookmaker Charlie Chisholm (far right) to bail them out in times of crisis. Trustees Savings Bank manager Dick McLaughlin was always there to offer sound financial advice. Another stalwart was Bart Conn, at the back, second from the right.

In 1964, a cricketing legend came to the land of pit heaps and winding gear. Langwell officials pulled off the greatest coup ever seen in local cricket when they managed to persuade top West Indian batsman, Rohan Kanhai, to throw in his lot with the coal-town squad. Making his debut against lowly Percy Main, Kanhai knocked a half-century in the twinkling of an eye. It was to be the first of many scintillating performances with the bat that was to bring crowds flocking into the ground to support the little team with the big ambitions. Photograph by Bob Johnson.

In spite of cricket being popular in Ashington, there was really only one game the lads wanted to play, and that was football. The Colliers soccer team even managed to get into the Football League Third Division in the 1920s and played in many stirring cup-ties. Ashington's captain Patrick O'Connel, in stripes, searches for his penny at Millwall's Den in 1922.

Even in the 1950s, the Black and Whites were pulling in the crowds at Portland Park. This is the famous cup-tie against Rochdale in 1950. Gordon Dent crosses the ball as two fans perch on top of the packed terraces.

Ashington FC team of 1946. Back row, from left to right: Tom Mason (masseur), Stan Milburn, C. Nesbitt, Ted Rutherford (goalkeeper), Raymond Poxon, C. Hepple, John Pop Dodd. Front row: Joe Meek, Jack Watson, Jackie Clough, Jim Sample, John Homer.

Footballing careers often began early. Ken Randall (back right) and Ken Prior (front right), with the 1946 Larry Bell Boys' Club team, played for Sheffield Wednesday and Newcastle United respectively.

The Hirst Park squad from 1950 included the rangy Jack Charlton, far right of the middle row. Kneeling in front of Jack is a former Newcastle United player, Bob Whitehead.

Lads progressed to junior level, like this squad which represented Ashington Welfare Juniors in a Cup Final at Portland Park against Seaton Delaval in 1955. From left to right, back row: Ron Bell, Jackie Cook, Ernie Wright, Andy Reay, Brian Nevins, Stan Laidlaw, John Lonsdale, Joe Grieve (coach). Front row: Brian Dixon, Colin Dobson, Colin Greener MP, Will Owen, Tom Baird, Colin Armstrong, Mr Major.

Larry Bell's Boys Club ran four soccer teams; this one played as the Midgets in 1947. The team includes Mike Parker (goalkeeper), Terry Davison, Hugh McDine, Jimmy Robertson and Keith Anderson.

Joe Grieve was involved with local football in one form or another for most of his working life. He began as an assistant groundsman under George Murdie at Ashington Rec. Joe is seen cutting the grass with his four-legged version of a flymo. He later went to Hirst Welfare as a groundsman before taking up the position of Welfare Organizer in 1968. There was always plenty to do at Hirst with the upkeep of football and cricket grounds, aided by assistants Tommy Douglas and Ted Hall. Joe initiated the Flower and Vegetable Show at the Welfare with Ernie Wallace as its first secretary, followed by Bob Coombs.

One man who made a habit of winning prizes for his vegetables at Hirst Welfare was Dickie Freeman, seen here at the Welfare in 1970. Born in 1923, Dickie's first garden was an allotment behind the Premier Club on Woodhorn Road. He was living then in the second block of Chestnut Street alongside Jackie Milburn. His best ever garden was an allotment at Woodhorn originally worked by Jack Douglas. So prolific was Dickie with his giant leeks that Tyne Tees television covered his exploits in a documentary.

It wasn't only the Milburns and Charltons who left Ashington to excel on the world footballing stage. Young Billy Gray could easily have been a professional boxer, having represented his country at youth level. However, he too became a footballer, playing for a number of top flight clubs, including Chelsea and Nottingham Forest, and he was honoured by his country when selected for an England B side. He is seen here at Portland Park in the 1960s, prior to playing in a benefit match.

Ashington had two schoolboy internationals in this East Northumberland team. Jimmy Jackson from the East School was honoured in 1948, and Percy Armstrong from the Park School gained his cap a year later. The team consisted of: Miller of Morpeth (in goal), Bill Robson, Sid Hutton (fullbacks), Jim Hill, Cyril Beddard, Jimmy Jackson (halfbacks), Graham of Newbiggin, 'Pud' Barnfather of Guide Post, Charlton of West Sleekburn, Percy Armstrong, 'Sam' Robinson (forwards). The latter two were both from the Park School

Jackie Milburn brought his four England caps into the Premier Club in 1948 and the steward, S. Dunn, showed them to his customers. Milburn went on to win thirteen caps in all.

It was the Ashington Welfare Football League who provided most of the city clubs with players. Additionally, it was the twenty workingmen's clubs in Ashington that organized teams to play in the League. The team above represented the Hirst Progressive in 1947 and scooped every prize. So they should; no less than five members of the team had played in the Football League. Can you spot them?

This was an outstanding Hirst Industrial team in 1949. From left to right, seated are: Charlie Anderson, Larry Lavelle, Danny Richardson, John Robinson, Tom Willis, Ned Tarbitt. Back row: Tom Davison, Albert Armstrong, Jim Taylor, Ren McLean, Bill Paxton, Des Mullholland, Nick Murray (trainer).

In the late 1950s it was the turn of Hirst East End Social Club to dominate the League and win silverware. The team consists of Ronnie Scott, Tom Liddell, Les Weddell, Tot Burns, John Smith, 'Pop' Anderson, Ernie Charlton, Ron Talbot, Percy Armstrong, Lol Carolyn and Law Weddell.

The Booth Cup originated in the early 1920s when Hirst Welfare was laid. During the 1926 miners' stoppage, local men and boys volunteered to wheel ash in barrows from Hirst Park to the Welfare where it was used to form No. 1 Pitch. The man who gave his name to the cup, Fred Booth, is seen in bowler hat, kicking off the inaugural match in August 1926.

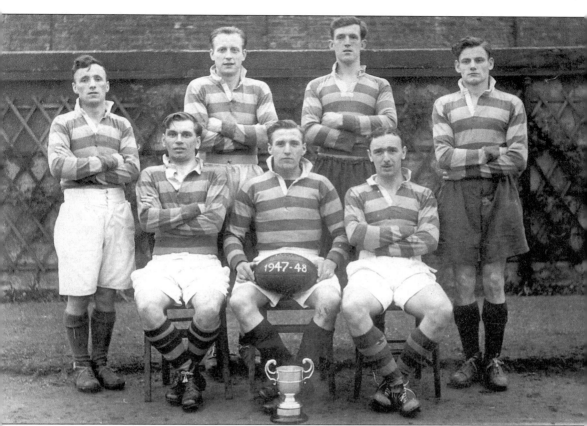

Ashington Rugby Club, although not enjoying the high profile of its round-ball counterparts, has, in the past few years, seen something of a renaissance. Squads have been strengthened, and it seems that Ashington is the team that everyone wants to play for. The club has not always played at the Rec, initially the venue was down what was Piggy Moor Lonnen, known now as Lintonville, moving to its present ground in 1922. Colliery manager, Fred Booth's son played for the team as one of its founder members. The clubhouse used today was once the house of Ashington Colliery's policeman. Later it was taken over by Ashington Farms. Percy Bates and Tommy Noble are two of the names generally mentioned when old-time rugger players get together to discuss who exerted influence on the club in the past. Tommy arrived at Ashington Colliery in 1934 where he found work with the Fire and Rescue Brigade, later turning out for the seconds as soon as the Second World War ended. It was not so long after that when Ashington were the Northern Sevens winners with the above team. From left to right, back row: Freddie Spare, Bill Williams, Joe Harding, George Wells. Seated: Stan Leithead, Ed Mullins, Jack Parkin.

Boxing was another popular sport. This squad trained in the Premier Club in the 1930s. From left to right, back row: Tom Bacon, Larry Lavelle, Bob Parkinson, Joe Swinhoe. Middle row: Tommy O'Keefe, Andy McLaughlin, Joe Denwood. Front row: Kid Barnes, Bill McLaughlin, Nick Carr, Jack Bacon, J. Rogers.

There were a number of venues where boxing matches could take place. Until it burned down, the Princess Ballroom staged some fine fights. Regular inter-village bouts were also held at the Hirst Welfare. As the poster states, these events took place at the Arcade Hall shortly after the Second World War ended. Local man Jock McQuade took top billing. Representing Larry Bell's Boys Club were Ivor Dixon, M. Morpeth, J. Graham, Bill Gibson, Cecil Tapson and RAF title holder Sam Morgan. For St Aidan's was Bill Cole. Fighting for the Bevin Boy's Hostel was Eddie Brown, an Irish cruiserweight.

Like old soldiers, boxers never die, they simply get barred from the club for fighting! Tom O'Keefe, on the right, spars in front of some of his old posters while top-ranked boxer, Seaman Tommy Watson acts as referee.

And old footballers? Well, they come back to have reunions at Woodhorn Colliery Museum, like these men did in 1996. From left to right: Mike Kirkup, Sid McLean, Bill Southern, Ken Steven, Charlie Crowe from the Newcastle United FA cup-winning team of 1951, Bobby Cummings – a record goalscorer for Ashington FC and former team-mate Crowe, Ron Talbot, 'Sam' Robinson.

Mike Kirkup put his football boots away and picked up a pen to record the life and times of Jackie Milburn in 1990. Proceeds from the book are now stored in a Trust Fund which helps disadvantaged children like Paul Stearman of Cramlington, seen with Mike on the steps of St James' Park.

Seven

Coal

Ashington Colliery in 1920 was one of the largest mining concerns in Britain. There were three pits within a pit – the Duke, Carl and Bothal, each with its own workforce, each with its own winding gear. Underground workings spread far and wide under the green fields of East Northumberland, and the surface buildings covered many acres. Vast chimneys dominated the landscape, belching out acrid smoke that covered the town and blackened the housewives' Monday wash.

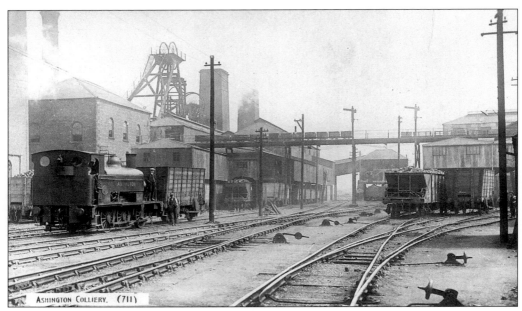

Ashington Colliery, seen here in the 1920s, was opened in 1867, shortly after the town's first pit at Fell 'em Doon failed. The colliery yard was only feet away from some of the back-to-back houses of its workforce.

For those who did have to travel, an open-sided train, called a tankey, was provided to take the miners to and from work. This one was called *Bothal*, and was probably on its maiden run, hence the men not being dressed for pitwork.

It soon became apparent that much time was being wasted by men travelling to their place of work, both above and below ground. This led to another mine being opened to the north, at Linton, in 1896.

As the workforce was being housed more and more at the Hirst end of town, it was only a matter of time before they too had a mine on their doorstep, at Woodhorn, drawing coals just before the turn of the century.

What a terrifying thing it was for a thirteen-year-old boy to go down the pit for the first time. Yet that was precisely what most of them were reared to do; the bigger the family, the more wage earners there would be. The coalowners looked forward to their annual intake of young lads. They were paid low wages and worked a minimum of twelve hours a day when Ashington Pit first began. It was sheer drudgery, with young boys not seeing the sunlight for days on end. How old do these mites look here in 1919? Twelve, perhaps. They carry their midgey lamp and wear the flat cap that makes men out of boys. By the look of their mucky faces, they have just come from the pit. Behind them gapes an open boley hole, ready to take a fresh load of coal into the cree. The lad second from the right is Billy Scott, born in 1906, died in 1972. He and his marraas (mates) lived in Juliet Street.

'Rap her away, hinney' and the banksman signals to the winding engineman that men are about to ride in the cage. Don't dare to call it a lift, or the muscular pitman who is scrushed next to you will carry your head off your shoulders. Down you go into the depths of Hell itself, perhaps never to see the light of day again.

Which is precisely what happened to thirteen men on Sunday 13 August 1916 at Woodhorn Colliery. They were a special team sent in to drive a new roadway in the Main Seam, clocking on at 6 a.m. Within an hour they were all dead, killed by an explosion of methane gas. It was a disaster waiting to happen as the gas had been allowed to accumulate over the weekend because a ventilation fan had been switched off for maintenance. At the subsequent Inquest the management was cautioned to be more careful. The widows were allocated three hundred pounds compensation and were later evicted from their colliery houses. No welfare state in those days.

In any situation like this it is always the children who suffer. The untimely death of Ned Walton, a stoneman aged forty-seven of Rosalind Street, left eight bairns, ranging from grown-up son William serving in the Armed Forces to two-year-old Adrian Joseph. Mrs Walton escaped being evicted by taking in two Irish lodgers who worked at the pit. The late Nance Walton (later Mrs Robson), who supplied this information and the photograph, is seated on the left.

From 1914 the Durham and Northumberland Fire and Rescue Brigade was housed on Station Bridge, next to the council offices. Initially working for the Coal Company, they later took on the role of fire fighters for the whole town.

Royalty paid a visit to Ashington Coal Company in 1928 in the shape of the Duke of York (left), later to become King George VI.

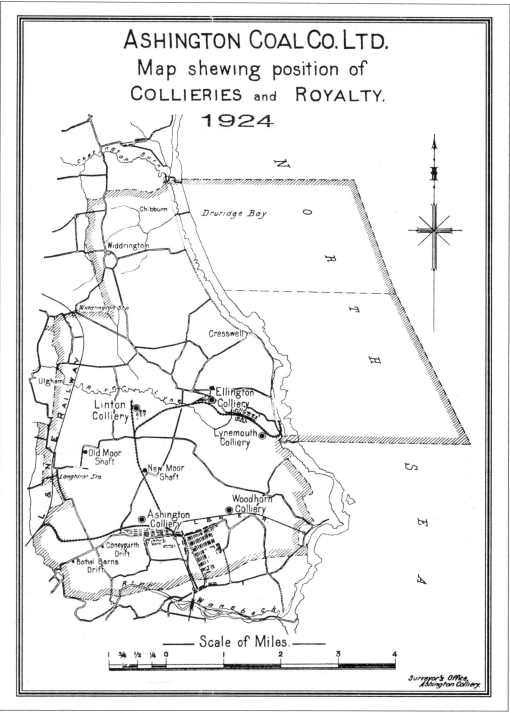

ASHINGTON COAL CO. LTD.
Map shewing position of
COLLIERIES and ROYALTY.
1924

Cresswell Burn

Chibburn

Druridge Bay

N O R T H   S E A

Widdrington

Widdrington Stn.

Cresswell

Ulgham

Ellington Colliery

Linton Colliery

Lynemouth Colliery

Old Moor Shaft

New Moor Shaft

Longhirst Stn.

Woodhorn Colliery

Ashington Colliery

Coneygarth Drift

Bothal Barns Drift

R. Wansbeck

L. & N.E. RAILWAY

L. & N. E. R.

Scale of Miles.

1 3/4 1/2 1/4 0   1   2   3   4

Surveyor's Office, Ashington Colliery.

Map of collieries belonging to the Ashington Coal Company in 1924. Much of the best coal was under the seabed.

Free coal was delivered to the miners' houses, in the first instance by horse and bogey. In the 1930s motor wagons were introduced. Larry Bell, then a second man, leans on the cab.

This sit-up-and-beg Foden is being cleaned out in the pit-yard next to the 11th Row by Jim Maxwell in 1940. Each wagon carried five loads of coal, weighing around half a ton each. The coal was dropped outside the boley hole in the back street next to the miners' cree (coalhouse) and 'hoyed' in by lads who did no other kind of work. Sixpence a load was the going rate in the '40s.

The putters of Ashington Colliery in the 1940s worked with pit ponies, providing fillers with empty tubs and taking full ones away. It was on a piecework rate basis and brought the young lad of eighteen a certain amount of prestige and a feeling of one-upmanship on the humble shifter. You can sense the swagger oozing out of every pore in Mel Harrison's body, as he leans on the backyard wall with a Robson Green smile on his face, slush cap at a suitably rakish angle on the head, carbide lamp hanging from lapel and one hand stuffed provocatively inside the belt. A typical young sparky pitman putter, at ease with himself and the world.

There is no spark in these tired eyes. It has been snuffed out by years of toil a thousand feet from the light of day. They sit at the bottom of the shaft, patiently, at the end of their shift. It does no good to hurry when you are this age. The year is 1954 and the mines were nationalised seven years ago. Yet conditions have barely improved. Men and boys are still killed or maimed every day, whereas the coal dust these men have breathed for the last thirty or forty years has yet to take its toll. From left to right: Jim Tait, Jack Smith, Ned Hodge, Jim Little, Jack Swanson.

Pit Props & Petticoats was the title of Jack Wallace's first book of short stories. There isn't a man better qualified to talk about either topic! A hard-working miner by day, Jack knew how to drag the most out of life away from the pulley wheels. He almost became a full-time photographer and he was a full-time concert chairman at the West End club, rubbing shoulders with Tyne Tees Television celebrities in the swinging sixties. Now retired, the wear and tear of the coalmine has caught up with the once energetic Jack the Lad. But the stories are there to be remembered.

Duke Street Coal Depot was responsible for sending out concessionary coal to every house in the Wansbeck area. It was also used for storing and selling house coal to merchants, such as Yard Seam Best and Bothal House Cobbles. A familiar sight in the depot yard was George Beaty's horse and cart, plus driver Geordie Nichol, seen with yard foreman Geordie Charlton.

The depot opened in the early 1930s with Jimmy Little as boss. In the beginning it was a cosy little office for two clerks, with a massive fireplace burning only the best coal standing at one side. Billy Mason and Mike Kirkup are pictured in 1962, by which time the living fire had gone (replaced by night-storage heaters) and six male clerks including Stu Sinclair, Tommy Tinkler, John Foster and Terry Saunders were packed in like sardines.

This 1950s aerial view shows just how close the colliery rows stood to the pit in the background, with its spoil tips ranging almost a mile long. Duke Street Depot is just off to the right, not visible.

If the camera taking that aerial shot could have zoomed in it would probably have caught sight of these Ashington Colliery blacksmiths and strikers hard at work.

Lads started a training scheme at Ashington at fifteen years of age. From left to right, back row: -?-, George Storey, -?-, Brian Blair, Ray Logan. Middle row: Bill Southern, ? Ramsden, Joe Darbyshire, Geordie Watson, Alan Ford, Mike Kirkup. Front row: Les McGowan, John Glasper, George Crate, -?-, Don Henderson, Bob York, Isaac Appleby, Jim Whitworth.

Young pit trainees in the 1950s had to learn every aspect of pit life. Putting a Gallowa into limmers for the first time could prove awkward. Pit ponies were worked extensively in all of Ashington pits where small workings rendered machines useless. Over 2,000 ponies worked at any one time in the 1920s. The last four ponies came to bank in 1994 when Ellington Colliery closed.

You can tell by their faces that these five likely lads are coming *out* of the pit in 1950. The Ashington Colliery men were, from left to right: Frankie Glasper, Jack Wallace, Billy Moffatt, Alan Armstrong, Geordie Roy.

These were nervous smiles on the faces of Ashington's Central Townswomen's Guild members in 1950. Training official Jack Crook gives them some last minute instructions before they venture underground into the pit.

Jack Campbell of Milburn Road had a dream in 1949; he wanted Woodhorn Colliery miners to have 3d levied from their pay to start their own brass band. That dream came to fruition, as seen in 1954. Among those pictured on the back row are: Jack Locker, John Tully, Ken Walton, Jack Pawlyn, Archie Locker, Sid Smith and Johnnie Reay. Included among those seated are: Jack Campbell, Stephen Howard and Ernie Johnson.

Up until 1952, miners had always taken the grime of the pit home with them. It was a common sight for half-naked men to be seen bent over a tin bath in the living room while their wives scrubbed at the parts of their body that a loofah couldn't reach. Geordie Bewick is seen with two of his marraas walking over Station Bridge in the 1930s. Each of the men has a carbide lamp hanging from lapel. The two on the left have their hoggers cut short at the knee.

Pit trainees in the early 1940s were deemed to be underweight and undernourished. As part of the bait-time they were given a free bottle of milk in Ashington Canteen, which opened in 1923 with Charles Sewell as the manager.

Duke Street Coal Depot saw many staff come and go, but Billy Mason (centre) must have served for the best part of forty years. Tommy Tinkler (second from the right) was originally a second man on the coal wagons before going to Woodhorn weighcabin. He was transferred to Duke Street in the 1960s. On the far right is Billy's brother, John Mason.

Ashington Area Central Workshops opened in 1961. Soon it was employing hundreds of men, handling and maintaining machines above and below ground in Northumberland.

One of the main reasons the miners' strike failed in the 1980s was because millions of tons of coal were stockpiled all around the country. Here Arthur Taylor, using a Dragline digger, around 1960, empties coal into NCB wagons for shipment from fields near Lynemouth.

The pits at Lynemouth, Linton and Woodhorn had already ceased to operate when the bitter strike of 1984 to '85 hammered the last nails into the coffin of Ashington Colliery. The Ashington men went back to work, beaten but unbowed, headed by the present council leader, John Devon. The poignancy is in the simple message of the children's misspelt banner.

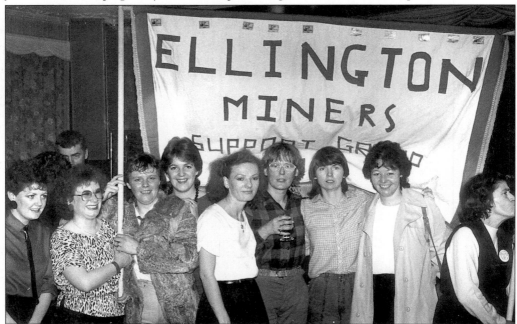

It was the Ellington miners' wives who showed solidarity in 1985. From left to right: Pat Maughan, Brenda Cunningham, Ann Foggerty, Jacqui Thompson, Karen Kull (a London girl), Linda Tench, Gwen Newton, Norma Kull. Ellington was the last colliery in the Ashington group to close in 1994, reopening a year later under private ownership.